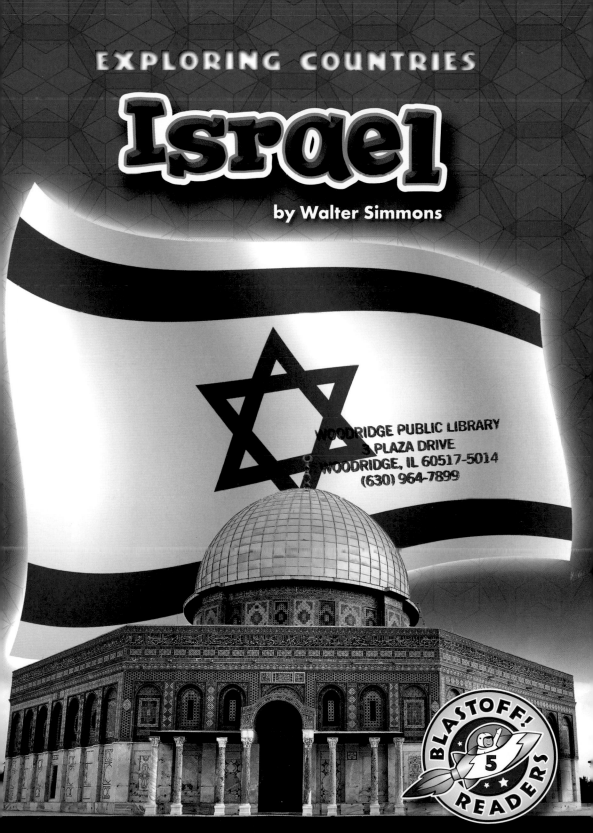

EXPLORING COUNTRIES

Israel

by Walter Simmons

BLASTOFF! 5 READERS

BELLWETHER MEDIA • MINNEAPOLIS, MN

Note to Librarians, Teachers, and Parents:

Blastoff! Readers are carefully developed by literacy experts and combine standards-based content with developmentally appropriate text.

Level 1 provides the most support through repetition of high-frequency words, light text, predictable sentence patterns, and strong visual support.

Level 2 offers early readers a bit more challenge through varied simple sentences, increased text load, and less repetition of high-frequency words.

Level 3 advances early-fluent readers toward fluency through increased text and concept load, less reliance on visuals, longer sentences, and more literary language.

Level 4 builds reading stamina by providing more text per page, increased use of punctuation, greater variation in sentence patterns, and increasingly challenging vocabulary.

Level 5 encourages children to move from "learning to read" to "reading to learn" by providing even more text, varied writing styles, and less familiar topics.

Whichever book is right for your reader, Blastoff! Readers are the perfect books to build confidence and encourage a love of reading that will last a lifetime!

This edition first published in 2011 by Bellwether Media, Inc.

No part of this publication may be reproduced in whole or in part without written permission of the publisher. For information regarding permission, write to Bellwether Media, Inc., Attention: Permissions Department, 5357 Penn Avenue South, Minneapolis, MN 55419.

Library of Congress Cataloging-in-Publication Data

Simmons, Walter (Walter G.)
 Israel / by Walter Simmons.
     p. cm. — (Exploring countries) (Blastoff! readers)
 Includes bibliographical references and index.
 Summary: "Developed by literacy experts for students in grades three through seven, this book introduces young readers to the geography and culture of Israel"—Provided by publisher.
 ISBN 978-1-60014-484-4 (hardcover : alk. paper)
 1. Israel—Juvenile literature. I. Title.
 DS118.S555 2010
 956.94—dc22   2010013662

Printed in the United States of America, North Mankato, MN.

080110   1162

Contents

Where Is Israel?

Lebanon

Syria

Mediterranean
Sea

Jordan
River

West
Bank

Gaza
Strip

Jerusalem ☆

Dead
Sea

Israel

Egypt

Jordan

Did you know?

The narrowest part of Israel,
between the Mediterranean Sea
and the West Bank region, is just
9 miles (14 kilometers) wide.

Gulf of
Aqaba

Israel is a nation in the **Middle East** that borders the Mediterranean Sea. It is a small country, spanning only 8,522 square miles (22,072 square kilometers). Lebanon is Israel's neighbor to the north, and Syria borders Israel to the northeast. Jordan lies to the east, across the Jordan River and the Dead Sea. Israel borders Egypt to the southwest, and in the south, it touches the **Gulf** of Aqaba. Jerusalem is the capital of Israel.

Israelis as well as Palestinians live in the **West Bank**, between Israel and the west bank of the Jordan River. The **Palestinian Authority** governs parts of the West Bank and the **Gaza Strip**, a tiny stretch of coastland between Israel and Egypt.

Israel is a land of deserts, mountains, and valleys. The country's coast stretches for miles. Warm winds blow across the coast's flat, dry land. In the east, the coastal plains rise to the Judean Hills, where the air is cooler. Pine trees cover the hills and valleys in this part of Israel.

The Judean Hills slope down to the Jordan River Valley. The Jordan River flows south before emptying into the Dead Sea. Northern Israel is also known as Galilee. The Sea of Galilee lies at its eastern edge. In the northeast sits a hilly region called the Golan Heights.

fun fact

The Negev Desert covers the southern half of Israel. Water is scarce in the Negev, a region of rocky, brown plains and dry riverbeds called *wadis*.

Jordan River

Did you know?

The Dead Sea is eight times saltier than the ocean. Salt rises from the water and settles in piles along the shores, which makes it impossible for plants to grow. Fish and other animals cannot survive in the Dead Sea.

The shores of the Dead Sea lie about 1,320 feet (402 meters) below sea level. This is the lowest point of land anywhere on Earth. Water from the Jordan River flows into the sea, but no water flows out of the sea. In a dry year, the water **evaporates** and the level of the sea falls several feet.

The Dead Sea is one of the only bodies of water in the world that is mined. The sea contains many valuable **minerals**. Water from the Dead Sea is pumped into large ponds. These ponds hold the minerals that remain behind as the water evaporates. Machine harvesters skim and collect the minerals, then send them to shore.

fun fact

All of the salt in the Dead Sea makes the water very dense. Because of this, it is very easy for people to float on the surface!

kingfisher

Many animals live throughout Israel. Horned animals such as gazelles, ibexes, and the white oryx live in the deserts and grasslands. In Israel's forests and hills, wild boars, wolves, and some leopards roam. Hawks, falcons, eagles, and kingfishers fly overhead, hunting small animals.

Did you know?

Israel is an important stop for birds that migrate with the seasons. So many birds migrate through Israel that they often interfere with airplanes!

fire salamander

ibex

fun fact

About thirty kinds of wild bats live in Israel. Fruit bats are a problem for farmers because they eat crops. Nets are used to capture the bats, and loud sounds are used to drive them away!

fruit bat

Israel is also home to many **amphibians**. Fire salamanders, marsh frogs, green toads, and tree frogs live throughout the country. On the seacoasts, herons and spoonbills make their nests. Sea turtles, sharks, and hundreds of different fish swim in the coastal waters.

More than 7 million people live in Israel. Most have **ancestors** that were Jewish **immigrants** who came to Israel from other countries. Some left their homes to escape war, but many Jews have come to Israel to live among their people. Israeli law says that every Jewish family in the world has the right to move to Israel. Many Arab families, most of whom are Muslim, also live in Israel. Jews and Muslims live close to each other in the cities and in the countryside.

Speak Hebrew!

Jews in Israel speak Hebrew. It is written in a different alphabet than English. However, it can be written in English so you can read it out loud.

English	Hebrew	How to say it
hello	shalom	sha-LOHM
good-bye	lehitra'ot	le-heetrah-OT
yes	ken	ken
no	lo	low
please	bevakasha	be-va-kah-SHA
thank you	toda	to-DAH
friend (male)	khaver	HAH-ver
friend (female)	khavera	hah-ver-AH

Did you know?

The Bedouin people dwell in the deserts of Israel. Some still live like their nomadic ancestors, traveling though the deserts with small herds of camels, goats, donkeys, or sheep.

The people of Israel have busy lives. In Israel's cities, most people live in apartment buildings. The streets are packed, and people must fight heavy traffic to get to work or school. Israelis who live in cities shop at markets, malls, and small shops.

Life in the countryside moves more slowly. Some Israelis live on a *kibbutz*. This is a farming community with homes, its own schools, and small factories.

Many Jewish families gather together on Friday nights. At sundown, *Shabbat* begins. This is the Jewish holy day when families share big meals and relax. On Saturday, the streets are quiet and most businesses are closed. *Shabbat* ends when three stars can be seen in the night sky on Saturday.

Where People Live in Israel

countryside 8%

cities 92%

kibbutz

Israeli children start school when they are 6 years old. Elementary school lasts six years. Students learn history, Hebrew, math, science, and other subjects. Middle school and high school each take three years to complete. Most students finish high school when they are 18 years old. At the end of high school, students take the *bagrut*. This exam tests them on their knowledge of Hebrew, English, math, religion, history, **civics**, and reading and writing

There are separate schools for Arab children, who learn in Arabic instead of Hebrew. They study the language, culture, and history of the Arab people. Recently, schools have been built that teach students in both Arabic and Hebrew.

! fun fact

Every year, thousands of tourists flock to Elat, a resort town on the Gulf of Aqaba. Service workers make sure these visitors enjoy themselves as they sunbathe, bird-watch, scuba dive, or swim.

Israel is a busy, productive country. In the cities, **engineers** design computer parts, machinery, and other technical equipment. Factory workers use these designs to make products that are shipped around the world. Because many tourists come to Israel, most Israelis hold **service jobs**. They work in hotels, serve food at restaurants, or make travel plans for people to visit churches, shrines, and other holy places.

In the countryside, many Israelis find work as farmers and miners. Farmers grow vegetables and citrus fruits, or raise livestock for meat and dairy products. Miners dig up diamonds and other minerals from the earth.

Did you know?
Israeli engineers helped develop voice mail and the cell phone. They have also made big contributions to solar energy technology.

Where People Work in Israel

manufacturing 16%

farming 2%

services 82%

backgammon

Israelis have many ways to spend their free time. Chess and **backgammon** are favorite board games in Israel. Israelis especially enjoy playing these games in parks or at sidewalk cafés. In the evening after work, many Israelis walk outside to shop and talk with their friends. Others go to a play, movie, or concert. Some streets in Tel Aviv-Yafo and Jerusalem stay crowded late into the night.

Most Israelis also enjoy playing and watching sports. Soccer and basketball are popular throughout the country. On the coast of the Mediterranean, Israelis practice surfing and windsurfing.

fun fact

In 2004, windsurfer Gal Fridman won Israel's first Olympic gold medal.

Israelis enjoy fresh fruits, vegetables, and meat in almost every meal. Breakfast often includes eggs, yogurt, juice, cheese, bread, olives, and coffee. Lunch is the biggest meal of the day, while dinner is usually a lighter snack.

A favorite food is the *falafel* sandwich. This is a pita stuffed with tomatoes, onions, cucumbers, and balls of mashed chickpeas. Couscous is a dish of small grains often topped with lamb and vegetables. *Shashlik* is grilled meat on skewers, usually served with rice or on a bed of lettuce. Israelis enjoy salads with tomatoes, peppers, onions, cucumbers, and other ingredients. Many Israelis drink strong coffee after a meal.

shashlik

couscous with lamb

falafel **sandwich**

There are nine public holidays every year in Israel. The dates of these holidays depend on the Jewish calendar, which is set by religious traditions. The year begins in the fall, and the Jewish New Year celebration, or *Rosh Hashanah*, lasts for two days.

Yom Kippur is an important Jewish holiday. It is also known as the Day of Atonement. During this holiday, most Jews **fast** during the day. *Hanukkah* lasts eight days. Each night, a new candle is lit on a *hanukiah*. Independence Day is the biggest spring holiday. On this day, Israel celebrates its founding as a nation in 1948.

hanukiah

The Temple Mount

A large platform supported by four stone walls rises in the center of Jerusalem. This is the Temple Mount. It is an important holy site for both Jews and Muslims. This was the site of two famous Jewish temples that were destroyed long ago. Jews still pray at the Western Wall, an original part of the second temple. According to tradition, Jews should not walk on top of the Temple Mount. The Temple Mount shows the long history of Jerusalem and the faiths it represents. It reminds the people of Israel of their history, culture, and traditions.

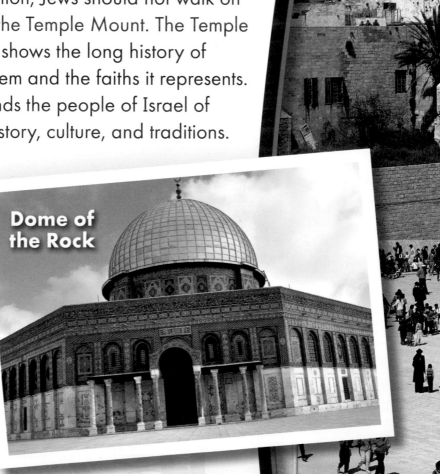

Dome of the Rock

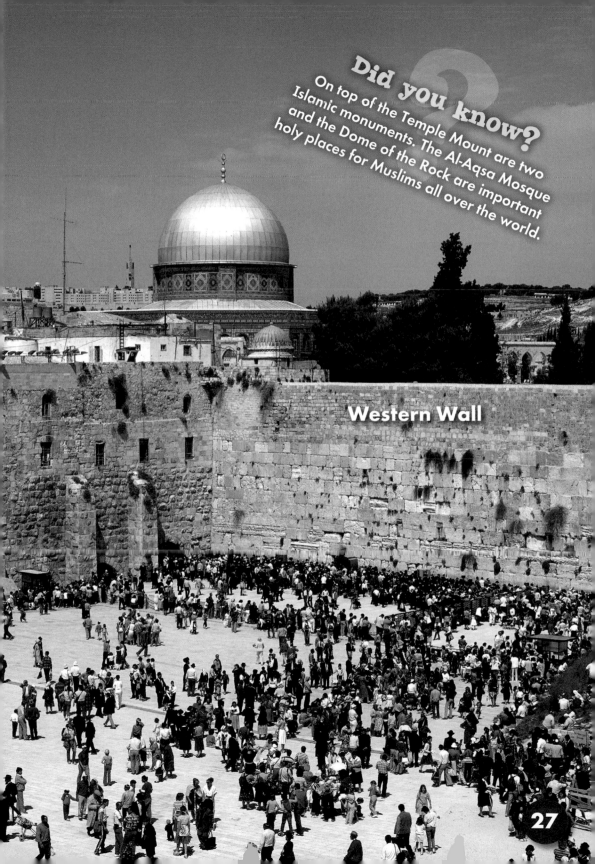

Western Wall

27

Fast Facts About Israel

Israel's Flag

The flag of Israel represents a traditional Jewish prayer shawl called a *tallit*. The background is white with two blue, horizontal stripes. In the middle of the flag is a blue, six-pointed Star of David. This is an old symbol of the Jewish religion and people. It is named for King David, an ancient king who won several important battles. The flag was adopted in 1948.

Official Name: State of Israel

Area: 8,522 square miles (22,072 square kilometers); Israel is the 152nd largest country in the world.

Capital City:	Jerusalem
Important Cities:	Tel Aviv-Yafo, Haifa
Population:	7,353,985 (July 2010)
Official Languages:	Hebrew and Arabic
National Holiday:	Independence Day (falls between April 15 – May 15)
Religions:	Jewish (76.4%), Muslim (16%), Other (7.6%)
Major Industries:	farming, manufacturing, mining, services
Natural Resources:	salt, phosphate, natural gas, clay, quartz, iron ore, diamonds
Manufactured Products:	clothing, computers, food products, machinery, chemicals, military equipment, cement, jewelry
Farm Products:	citrus fruits, corn, dates, flowers, potatoes, tomatoes, poultry
Unit of Money:	new Israeli shekel; the shekel is divided into 100 agorot.

Glossary

amphibians—cold-blooded animals that live in water and breathe with gills when they are young; when amphibians are adults, they live on land and breathe with lungs.

ancestors—relatives who lived long ago

backgammon—a game of skill and chance played with a board, pieces called checkers, and dice

civics—studies related to being a good citizen of a country or community

engineers—people who plan and build machines, buildings, and other structures

evaporates—changes from a liquid into a gas

fast—to choose not to eat

Gaza Strip—a small territory along the Mediterranean Sea, neighboring Israel to the southwest; the Gaza Strip is governed by the Palestinian Authority.

gulf—part of an ocean or sea that extends into land

immigrants—people who leave one country to live in another country

Middle East—a region of the world from the eastern part of the Mediterranean Sea to the western part of the Arabian Sea

minerals—elements found in nature; gold, silver, and iron are examples of minerals.

Palestinian Authority—the organization that governs parts of the West Bank and Gaza Strip

service jobs—jobs that perform tasks for people or businesses

West Bank—a territory between Israel and the Jordan River; Israel controls part of the West Bank, and the Palestinian Authority controls the other part.

To Learn More

AT THE LIBRARY

Hintz, Martin. *Israel*. New York, N.Y.: Children's Press, 2006.

Rivlin, Lilly, and Gila Gevritz. *Welcome to Israel*. Springfield, N.J.: Behrman House, 2000.

Waldman, Neil. *The Golden City: Jerusalem's 3,000 Years*. Honesdale, Penn.: Boyds Mills Press, 2000.

ON THE WEB

Learning more about Israel is as easy as 1, 2, 3.

1. Go to www.factsurfer.com.

2. Enter "Israel" into the search box.

3. Click the "Surf" button and you will see a list of related Web sites.

With factsurfer.com, finding more information is just a click away.

Index

The images in this book are reproduced through the courtesy of: Avner Richard, front cover, p. 26 (small); Maisei Raman, front cover (flag), p. 28; Jon Eppard, pp. 4-5; Roman Sigaev, pp. 6-7, 29 (coin); Scott Truesdale, pp. 6 (small), 11 (bottom), 22 (left), 29 (bill); Alex Gul, p. 8; JTB Photo/Photolibrary, p. 9; Poinsignon and Hackel/Nature Picture Library, pp. 10-11; Juniors Bildarchiv/Photolibrary, p. 11 (top); Rostislav Glinsky, p. 11 (middle); Jon Hicks/Getty Images, p. 12; Age Fotostock, p. 13; Lauree Feldman/Photolibrary, p. 14; Hanan Isachar/Photolibrary, p. 15; Dan Porges/Photolibrary, pp. 16, 19 (left); Caroline Penn/Photolibrary, p. 17; Jon Arnold Images Ltd/Alamy, p. 18; R Matina/Photolibrary, p. 19 (right); Alison Wright/Robert Harding/Getty Images, p. 20; Getty Images, p. 21; Brett Mulcahy, p. 22 (right); Eyal Nahmias/Alamy, p. 23; Mikhail Levit, pp. 24-25; GW Images, p. 25 (small); Steve Vidler/Photolibrary, pp. 26-27.